To _Courenie_

From _X ✱ ? ✱ X_

The Mini Book of
LOVE
SPELLS

DEBORAH GRAY

HarperCollins*Publishers*

*Believe in yourself
and the magical
power of love*

Deborah Gray

Deborah Gray

Australia's Good Witch was born into a long heritage of Celtic magic and mysticism. Initiated as a teenager into an Ancient Druid Circle, she has studied white witchcraft and alchemy for over twenty years, inheriting her knowledge of parapsychology and spellcasting from one of the world's few remaining Druid Masters. As the author and co-author of the international bestsellers, *Nice Girl's Book of Naughty Spells* and *How to Turn Your Ex-Boyfriend into a Toad,* Deborah is one of Australia's best known and respected writers. Her inspirational words of magic have been translated into four languages, exciting the imaginations of many thousands of people around the world. In addition to her busy schedule as a metaphysical lecturer and writing a weekly column for *New Idea* magazine, Deborah is passionately recreating the original perfumes and enchanted potions of ancient times. She has recently released her own Goddess of Love Potion.

To contact Deborah regarding her lectures, potions or catalogue, please write to:

PO Box 229, Woollahra, NSW 2025 Australia

website: www.deborahgraymagic.com

e-mail: witchg@mpx.com.au

HarperCollins*Publishers*

First published in Australia in 2000
by HarperCollins*Publishers* Pty Limited
ACN 009 913 517
A member of the HarperCollins*Publishers* (Australia) Pty Limited Group
http://www.harpercollins.com.au

HarperCollins*Publishers*
25 Ryde Road, Pymble, Sydney, NSW 2073, Australia
31 View Road, Glenfield, Auckland 10, New Zealand
77-85 Fulham Palace Road, London W6 8JB, United Kingdom
Hazelton Lanes, 55 Avenue Road, Suite 2900, Toronto, Ontario M5R 3L2
and 1995 Markham Road, Scarborough, Ontario M1B 5M8, Canada
10 East 53rd Street, New York NY 10022, USA

National Library of Australia Cataloguing-in-Publication data:

Gray, Deborah (Deborah Noelle).
The Mini Book of Love Spells: goddess magick for passion, love and seduction.
ISBN 0 7322 6669 6.
1. Magic - Humor. 2. Love - Humor. 3. Man-woman relationships - humor. I Title.
133.442

Printed in Australia by Mc Pherson's Printing Group on 79gsm Bulky Paperback
5 4 3 2 1   00 01 02 03 04

Contents

The Magick of Love

Love, glorious love!

Love is an emotion, and it is also a beautiful
energy that connects all living beings.
Love can take us to dizzying heights
of passion and excitement.
We all desire love. More than any other aspect of
our lives, our search for eternal love is the most
basic and strongest desire of all. Since time
began, spells have been cast and magic charms

created not only to help us find love, but also
to help us keep it. The true art of Love Magick
is about learning to connect with your natural
inner power and the mystical energies of the
infinite Universe – not about control or forcing
someone to love you. You deserve to love
and be loved – so cast a magic spell and
awaken the goddess within!

Who is your Guardian Goddess?

We have all heard of 'guardian angels', those wonderful angel guides who tap us on the shoulder when we need some spiritual advice, or help us in times of great stress or danger. But did you know that since ancient times many great civilisations also believed in 'guardian goddesses'?

While there will always be different goddesses for different needs and occasions, your guardian goddess is aligned with the vibrations of your deep subconscious and can guide you to awaken your true goddess nature and magical energy.

Look up your star sign on the following pages and see which guardian goddess can help you cast magic spells for passion, love and seduction.

Aries

The goddess MAIA personifies your Aries sense
of playfulness and sexy energy. Maia is the
goddess of fertility and fiery passion who
was honoured by the ancient Romans with
fabulous all-night toga parties and flower-
stomping festivals. She is the ideal goddess to
ensure that you always exude that special
enchanting glow, even when you've been
up dancing 'til dawn in your bare feet,
or if you're simply relaxing at home with your
chosen one – preferably sipping red wine
in front of a cosy fire.

Maia

Maia
Love Spell

YOU WILL NEED TO GATHER:

A red scarf or robe
An orange candle
Your favourite floral essence

Invoke the sizzling love power of Maia by draping a red scarf or robe over your shoulders. Light an orange candle anointed with your favourite floral essence, then sit in a comfortable position nearby.

Breathe deeply and concentrate on drawing loving energy towards you. Picture the goddess in your mind as you repeat this incantation:

'Weave your spell of silken thread,
Draped with deepest velvet-red,
Through cedar woods and ancient pine;
Surround me with love and romance divine.

O fairest Maia, goddess of desire,
Through indigo clouds of incense and fire,
Let her earthly guide be candle glow,
Into the temple may passion flow.'

Stay With Me

YOU WILL NEED TO GATHER:

Seven small stones
A cup of tarragon leaves
A box

If you'd like to attract a great guy (or girl) and you want this new love to last, help cement the relationship by casting this spell on the night of a new moon. Gather together seven small stones (they may be pebbles from a garden or crystals bought

from a shop) and a cup of tarragon leaves. Go to a quiet space in your home near a window. Place the stones clockwise in a circle around you while you think about your intended lover. Sprinkle the tarragon around in an anti-clockwise direction as you repeat this incantation:

> *'Solid to the right, strength is on the left,*
> *Our love will stay with the power of this*
> *The Magick Hour.'*

Finish the spell by remaining within the circle for a few minutes while you concentrate on visualising the two of you happy and in love. Leave the circle as it is overnight. In the morning, gather up the stones and tarragon and put them in a box to keep under your bed.

Taurus

Your goddess was worshipped in ancient Crete. Represented by the female bull, her name is TAUROPOLOS. Honoured for her strength and the ability to bring out lust in everyone, young men would line up, eagerly showing off their physical prowess by attempting somersaults through her magnificent horns. A warning though: her powers of attraction could be dangerously irresistible, so do be careful when you wear that sexy red underwear, or you may find yourself being chased around a paddock by a Latin gymnast!

Tauropolos

Tauropolos Love Spell

Ask the goddess Tauropolos to help bring love into your life by casting this spell on the night of a new or growing moon. Gather together some saffron powder, a pebble (one that you have found outside in a park or a garden) and a garnet crystal (available from crystal shops or new age stores).

Take a bath or shower to clear away any negative or stressful energy and put on some clean, natural-fibre clothing. Find a quiet, private space in your home and place the pebble and crystal on the floor in front of you. Sprinkle the saffron around you in a

clockwise circle as you concentrate on feeling the goddess energy. Repeat this incantation:

'See here now the saffron dust
Swirling at your feet,
Turning now to fiery jewels
And precious magic gems.
I look again – your secret name
Is carved in whitest stone.
I call on you Tauropolos, goddess of ancient Crete,
May romance knock upon my door
and love's delight be shown.'

Seal the spell's power by sweeping up the saffron with a broom. Place the items of enchantment in a wooden or cardboard box and keep it in your bedroom for at least a month.

Heart's Desire

When you are ready for someone new or to bring back a past love, cast this attraction spell on a fine morning of a new or waxing moon (when the moon is growing from new to full).

Begin by finding a safe place outside your home where you can see the front door or a front window. Take a handful of sesame seeds with you and stand for a few moments looking into the sky as you appreciate the different shades of blue and the different shapes and colours of any clouds above you. Fill your lungs with fresh air by taking a

number of deep breaths. Then sprinkle the sesame seeds near the front door and window of your home, repeating this incantation:

'My heart's desire will now fully bloom,
My true soul mate will be arriving soon.
As the seeds of magic begin to grow,
Through my door real love shall flow.'

Gemini

NIKE, goddess of expression and movement, is your perfect twin. She is a beautiful winged nymph who zooms through the skies at great speed and loves hanging out with her groovy goddess friends. Nike always makes sure she's invited to the best A-list parties in heaven. (Remember this whenever a snooty doorman is giving you problems!) Most importantly, Nike is the goddess of victory who always gets her man. Her energy aligns perfectly with your incredible zest for life and love of good company.

Nike

Nike Love Spell

YOU WILL NEED TO GATHER:

A silver ring or necklace
A white feather
A sprig of lavender

To invoke love and the power of Nike, gather
together your items of enchantment. At night, put
on the necklace or ring and hold the feather and
lavender in your hands. Stand near an open

window in your home, look into the sky and whisper this incantation to the night wind:

> *'Since time began to soar and fly,*
> *It is written on the wind:*
> *Fairest Nike shall bring success*
> *Sent on a goddess wing.*
> *Here this night I call on you*
> *To ensure love's destiny,*
> *May your enchantment light my way*
> *And bring eternal joy to me.'*

Seal the spell's power by breathing in the aroma of the lavender for a moment and then tossing both the feather and lavender out of the window.

Bliss Bath

YOU WILL NEED TO GATHER:

1 cup Epsom salts
½ cup baking soda
1 tablespoon dried lavender
1 teaspoon chamomile tea

Treat your own mind and body to some love magick
with this wonderful bath of bliss. Begin by mixing
up some 'bliss powder', using the ingredients above.

Mix together the ingredients in a large bowl and
let them stand for one hour. If you wish, you can

also add a few drops of your or favourite essential oil. Then put everything into a jar with a lid. Draw a warm bath and pour in a few tablespoons of the 'bliss powder'. Soak in the bath while you relax your body and mind completely.

Cancer

SELENE is the ancient Roman goddess of the moon and emotional love. Her skin glimmers like silver – legend has it that she carefully bathes in the sea at sunset before travelling across the night sky in a glistening chariot to woo her admirers with wondrous poetry and romance. With your love of expensive perfumes and candlelit baths, Selene is the perfect goddess for you to call upon before you invite your lover over for a seductive night of moonlit passion.

Selene

Selene Love Spell

Empower yourself with the energy of the goddess Selene with this ancient bathing ritual. Perform this ritual on a night before a hot date, or whenever you feel like boosting your powers of attraction.

Take some time out to pamper yourself with a lovely bubble bath or fragrant shower. Remain in the shower or bath for a few moments as you imagine that Selene's energy is shining through to you and filling you with her enchanted power. Then, after you dry yourself, anoint your body with a lightly perfumed body cream as you repeat this incantation:

'Sylphs and elves gather to see,
That goddess Selene shall hearken to me.
Hear my plea in night's quietest hour,
Let your moonlight glisten with silvery power.
May each dusk and dawn
Bring me love's true glimmer,
For it shall be so and so will it be.'

Chocolate Heart Spell

YOU WILL NEED TO GATHER:

A heart-shaped box of chocolates
Lavender cologne
A red ribbon

Spice up the time-honoured gift of a beautiful box of chocolates with some seduction sorcery. Before you give it to your intended, place the box of chocolates on a small table, then walk clockwise once around in a circle as you lightly spray a fine mist of lavender

cologne in the air. Next, stand near the table facing east, breathe calmly for a few minutes and repeat this incantation:

> *'Spirit of the eastern sun*
> *Now my charming has begun,*
> *All true beauty that lies within,*
> *Seal this spell with love to win.*
> *In the name of good it will be done.'*

Finish the spell by tying a red ribbon around the box of chocolates.

Leo

Just like you, BAST is the original sex kitten. This
Egyptian goddess understands the joy of the hunt,
and she aligns perfectly with your sexy feline
psyche. It is said that just one look from her golden
almond eyes can entice anyone she chooses.
A favourite goddess among the women of
Nefertiti's time, Bast is an ancient solar deity
who also takes the form of a cat or lion.
She particularly enjoys playfully toying with
her lovers before she finally captures them.
(Sound familiar?)

Bast

Bast Love Spell

YOU WILL NEED TO GATHER:

A tiger's eye crystal
A leopard-print or tiger-print scarf
A stick of musk incense

To help bring romance and the energy of the goddess Bast into your love life, gather together your items of enchantment. At 7 o'clock on any night, light the incense and wrap the animal-print scarf around you. Hold the crystal in both hands

and breathe deeply and calmly for a few moments.
Concentrate on attracting love toward you and
picture the goddess in your mind as you say these
magic words:

'O goddess, I see you gaze through golden eyes;
So silently you speak your words.
A delicate stroll through crystal sands,
Curling through perfumed corridors,
Now let this ancient alchemy awaken you O Bast,
Let my desire for sacred love come to me at last.'

Honeymoon Magic

To bless a new relationship, invite your lover over for supper. A few hours beforehand, purchase or make your own apple cake mix. Blend the ingredients together in a big china bowl and pour the mixture into a baking tin. Sprinkle in a touch of cinnamon and a teaspoon of honey as you repeat this incantation:

'This blessed moon cake that I bake,
Fill up with goodness for everlasting sake.'

After the cake has finished baking, allow it to cool and then hold it up towards the moonlight as you think about your new love and repeat the incantation three more times. When you serve the cake to your lover, don't cut it with a knife or any other cutting tool (this will cut the spell's power). Instead, break off small pieces with your hands and romantically feed the cake to him and then to yourself. Serve with lashings of honey or apple butter for a night of sweet love.

Virgo

Often thought of as an earthy forest nymph, you are also influenced by the star goddess, ASTRAEA. She became bored with earthly pursuits and rose elegantly into the sky to form the constellation of Virgo. Astraea believes in fair play and loyalty, but no man should ever underestimate her gentle nature, or she will be gone in a shimmering flash of stardust. Just like you, she can just as easily enjoy flying away on her own (preferably first-class) to somewhere exotic and fabulous if she needs some extra stimulation and excitement.

Astraea

Astraea Love Spell

YOU WILL NEED TO GATHER:

A peridot or green crystal
Geranium-scented body oil
A small make-up mirror
A pretty gift box
A piece of blue paper

All goddesses adore beautiful presents, so attract
love and Astraea into your home by making her a
special magic box. Gather together a peridot or a

green crystal (available at new age and crystal shops), a small vial of geranium-scented body oil, and a small make-up mirror. Wrap everything in tissue and put it into a pretty gift box. Sit down and write these words on a piece of blue paper:

> *'O goddess Astraea, send me the gift of love*
> *And linger here awhile,*
> *For behold within this magic box*
> *You'll find enchanted fare.*
> *A crystal to shine and light your day*
> *With a secret oil to smooth your care*
> *And a looking glass to guide your way.'*

Put the paper in the box, put on the lid and leave it near your bedroom window for as long as you wish.

Que Sera Sera

Two pink candles
Essence of jasmine
Two candle holders
A new notebook

When you want to attract your perfect match, this spell works very well if you concentrate not just on physical appearance, but also on personality and character.

Cast your love spell on the night of a full moon by anointing two pink candles with some essence of jasmine and placing them in holders on either side of a new notebook. Light the candles and sit nearby so you can write down these magic words:

'I call on one who is happy and wise,
Who looks at me with sparkling eyes.
And in his sight I can do no wrong,
For our love is right and true and strong.
So shall the Universe hear my request.'

When you have finished writing, look at the words and in your mind's eye, concentrate on seeing your new lover and try to feel yourself holding him and sending him your affection and thoughts. Repeat the spell once a week for at least a month.

Libra

HATHOR, the Egyptian goddess of art, femininity and beauty, is a wonderful flirt who enjoys lilting music and playing to an audience. So, when you next feel the urge to dance on top of the restaurant table, you'll know it's because your guardian goddess often cheered up the moody gods with an impromptu belly dance around the heavens. Hathor's powers of seduction are among the strongest of all the goddesses, so she's very handy to call on to give you a sexy boost after a hard day of balancing your life (and everyone else's!)

Hathor

49

Hathor Love Spell

YOU WILL NEED TO GATHER:

Flower petals
Glitter
Morris bells

Attract love and celebrate your connection with the goddess Hathor by having a little private dance party in her honour. Sprinkle lots of pretty flower petals and glitter over the floor and tie some traditional Morris bells around your wrists and ankles for extra magic

during your goddess dance. You can make Morris bells by threading a few small craft bells onto some lengths of pink or red ribbon, and tying them around your ankles with a bow. (Craft bells are available in haberdasheries and pet shops.)

Put on some of your favourite music and dance around your bedroom or living room as you say aloud:

'O beautiful Hathor, goddess of love,
Send me romance and luck from above.
Let ancient drums beat and ringing bells sound,
Come dance with me as the finest ribbons fly.
Gently walk among Earth's scented flowers,
Shower me from the heavens with love's
sacred power.'

Cupid's Dart

What better way of meeting someone new than holding a party for a number of your friends – making sure, of course, that they invite some of their other friends. This will give you the perfect opportunity to place symbols of togetherness and love discreetly around the rooms to stimulate romantic interest and lots of fun.

The best time to throw the party would be on a Friday evening. Prepare beforehand some plates of passion power food such as fresh fruit and handfuls

of chocolates and nuts. Place these around your
home for romantic nibbles. You may set any tables
with a white tablecloth and make a lovely display of
red and white scented flowers. Then, just before
your guests arrive, walk clockwise around the main
room and say:

'Goddess Venus call Eros here tonight,
If love can start may Cupid's dart find its path.'

Scorpio

The mysterious SERKET is one of the most
ancient Egyptian goddesses, who also aligns
beautifully with your deep understanding of
mysticism and karma. She loves exploring
secret and out-of-the-way places and playing sexy
mind games with her chosen lovers. You will
definitely relate to her way-out dress sense – she
loves to wear a stunning scorpion-shaped
headdress – and her passionate sense of her
own seductive spiritual power.

Serket

Serket Love Spell

YOU WILL NEED TO GATHER:

A small white party candle
A small purple party candle
Musk oil

To invoke love and your inner goddess power, gather two small party candles – a white one to represent yourself and a purple one for Serket. Place the candles in the centre of a table in holders or on a dish. Dab a little musk oil onto both candles. Next, light them both and repeat this incantation:

'I light the flame of mystery
For you, O goddess Serket,
To unlock the secret pathways
through the magic of ancient Egypt.
As you follow the flickering golden light
Of this enchanted fire,
May you surround me now
With the wonders of love and
passion's true desire.'

Gaze at the lit candles while you let go of stress and negative thoughts. Watch the candles burn down until the flame goes out and just the wax remains. Leave everything on the dish to cool overnight. In the morning, bury the melted wax in a garden or flowerpot.

Totally Devoted

YOU WILL NEED TO GATHER:

Two lengths of string, about 30 cm long
A stick of geranium or ylang ylang incense
Something your intended lover
has touched, eg pen or paper
A handful of rose petal potpourri

If you want to bring a loved one closer to you,
collect together these items of enchantment on
Friday, the day of Venus. Wrap one of the lengths

of string around the stick of incense at the base and keep wrapping all the way up to the tip as you focus your mind on your intended and say:

> *'I bind this chord to show my love,*
> *I bind this chord to start desire.'*

Put the item your loved one has touched next to the incense and start wrapping that up with the other piece of string. After you have wrapped everything up, sprinkle the rose petals over the top. For added passion, keep everything under your bed for at least a month.

Sagittarius

If you can picture yourself dressed in gold on a dazzling white steed, your hair flying in the wind, then the equine goddess of ancient Gaul, EPONA, is the girl for you. She is fiercely independent, but never knocks back a chance to race some of the fastest men in the west to the finish line. Just like you, Epona is full of surprises and when she does decide to give a guy a break and let him catch her, she lets down her flowing mane and entertains her rapt audience with amazing imitations of lusty bird songs.

Epona

Epona
Love Spell

YOU WILL NEED TO GATHER:

Aloe vera gel
A leather belt
A natural-bristle brush

To invoke the love power of the goddess Epona,
collect your spell items on the week of a waxing
(growing) moon. At 8 o'clock on any evening, take a
luxurious bath or shower. After you have patted
yourself dry, anoint your whole body with the aloe

as you concentrate your mind on thoughts of love and romance. Remain undressed and wrap the leather belt around your waist. Gently brush your hair as you look into a mirror and repeat this magic incantation:

'Hearken now and ride alongside the unicorn,
Let's stop to drink at love's sweet well.
Lie among Apollo's garden of meadow fern;
I call you here O wild Epona.
Come show me again the highest magic realm,
This enchanted land where passion is born.'

After your ritual, keep the belt and the brush in a special corner of your bedroom.

Enchanted Gift

What better symbol of love than a beautiful handmade gift. This lucky talisman is easy to make and it's a wonderful magic charm for a lover or friend.

Find a nicely shaped light-coloured pebble or small stone and a blue indelible marker pen. Wash and dry the stone, then hold it to your 'third eye chakra' – between your eyes – as you visualise a golden light shining from your chakra, and flowing into the stone. Then think of things your loved one desires and needs most in their life. Choose one

and, as you concentrate strongly on that, repeat this incantation:

> *'May this stone help their dream come true,*
> *With loving and generous energy,*
> *By the ancient rule of three times three,*
> *May this now be done so mote it be.'*

Finally, draw the number '7' onto the stone. Place it in a little satin or homemade cotton pouch in your loved one's favourite colour for an inspiring magical gift from your heart.

Capricorn

The Roman nymph ALMATHEIA once
nourished Zeus, king of the gods, with goat's milk
and honey. A cheeky and ambitious goddess,
she was rewarded with the gift of everlasting
success and tenacity and the ability to sustain the
world. Almatheia's feisty energy fits right in
with your Capricornian talent for whipping up a
post-l'amour meal out of the one egg and leftover
champagne in your fridge. (Although your lover
probably needs a bit more nourishing than that
to keep up with your incredible stamina!)

Almatheia

Almatheia Love Spell

YOU WILL NEED TO GATHER:

A cup of goat's milk
A sprig of fresh mint
Jasmine-scented body oil

To bring love and the power of Almatheia toward
you, cast this spell on the day of Saturn, Saturday.
Find a time in the day or evening when you can be
undisturbed for a while and place all your spell items
in your bathroom. Take a relaxing shower or, better

still, a bath. While you are bathing, smooth some of
the body oil over you while you think of your love
wish. After bathing, dry yourself and pour the goat's
milk into a cup. Add the fresh mint to the goat's milk.
Take a sip, then repeat this incantation:

> *'Let me bathe with you, O sacred one*
> *In the nectar of the Gods.*
> *Let the coolest mint soothe your brow*
> *As you sip the milk of love.*
> *Let scented oils bring you near*
> *O goddess Almatheia;*
> *Send me the elixir of romance and laughter*
> *And a joyous dream so dear.'*

Finish the spell by drinking the goat's milk and the
mint. Repeat the incantation as often as you like.

Bubble Bubble

YOU WILL NEED TO GATHER:

A cauldron or metal bowl
Two silver candles
One maroon candle
Jasmine incense
A wooden stick

You've seen the guy you want, you just have to get his attention! Leave your magic cauldron or metal bowl near a window to be charged by the moon overnight.

On the next night, place the bowl on a table between two silver candles. Place a maroon candle in the bowl by melting the end of the candle slightly with a match so it sticks firmly to the bottom of the bowl. Light some jasmine incense and two silver candles. With the wooden stick in your right hand, gently tap the side of the bowl three times as you say the words:

> *'One to reach him, two to bring him,*
> *Three to keep him near.'*

Tap the cauldron with the stick three more times. Light the maroon candle as you picture your intended lover in your mind, focusing on loving thoughts. Seal the spell's power by snuffing out the candles and saying:

> *'Devoted we'll be, together as one,*
> *It shall be so, this spell is done'.*

Aquarius

You are aligned with the Egyptian sky goddess, NUUT, the personification of heavenly love power. Her sensuous body is painted with stars and she is able to reach out with her delicate fingers and toes to touch the four cardinal points of the world. (No wonder you can so easily stretch your credit card limit to the north, south, east and west!) Her spiritual energy fits perfectly with the inventive way you can think of three lovers at once and your eerie ability to attract interesting lovers from faraway places.

Nunt

Nuut Love Spell

YOU WILL NEED TO GATHER:

Three floating silver candles
Rose incense
Sugar
A bowl of water

To call in romance and the power of the goddess Nuut, you could try a little love magic by casting this spell on a Friday, preferably during a new or waxing (growing) moon. Place three floating silver candles in

a bowl of water. Light the candles and one stick of rose incense. Sit nearby as you focus your thoughts on romance and love while gently inhaling the aroma of the incense. Next, sprinkle a tiny amount of sugar into the bowl of water as you repeat this incantation:

'I stir, I mix, I manifest the energy of Goddess Nuut.
These words I speak, this magic spell
Her power will invoke.
I stir, I mix, I manifest the casting has begun;
A thousand stars adorn her O the Ancient One;
May joy now fill my waking hours
And all my sleep-filled nights.
Send me all my heart's desire
And love that's true and right.'

Matchmaker

To encourage your intended lover to think of you,
either find a photograph of him or write his name
on a clean piece of paper twelve times. Stick it
face-down on a small make-up mirror. Then write
the following words on the back of a photograph
of yourself:

'By these magic words I make this plea,
When you see your reflection
You will think of me.'

Stick the photo on the back of the mirror face-down. Hold the mirror in your hand and concentrate with all your might on visualising your intended's face. Repeat the same incantation aloud three times.

Keep the mirror in your purse or pocket for at least a month.

Pisces

ISIS is the Egyptian Goddess of High Magic. Her
dreamy soul and psychic powers match
perfectly with your Piscean spiritual awareness, but,
like you, she can also be the ultimate love diva.
Her powers are legendary – she was one of the first
girls to use glamour and magic spells to entice
her lovers. Her apprentice was the naughty
Cleopatra, who seduced Mark Antony and Julius
Caesar with a lot of help from the magic of Isis.
So, if you can get this goddess on your team, your
dreams of running off with your perfect lover
are not too far off.

Isis

Isis Love Spell

YOU WILL NEED TO GATHER:

A few strands of your own hair
Three camellia or carnation petals
A small amethyst crystal

Use the power of your dreams to bring love and the goddess Isis into your magic realm. Take a few strands of your own hair (a few from your comb or brush will do fine), plus the camellia or carnation petals and amethyst crystal. Set up a special altar to

Isis in your bedroom by placing your spell items on
a pretty table. Hold the amethyst in your hand and
focus on feelings of love and happiness as you
repeat this incantation:

> *'Goddess Isis, lady of the ancient way,*
> *Carry my message through the call of the spirit*
> *Along the sacred river Nile.*
> *Hear me whisper in your dreams*
> *Among the rustling reeds of long-forgotten times.*
> *Hasten now and awaken me to precious love*
> *Throughout the night and day.'*

Place the petals, hair and crystal under your pillow
and repeat this spell as often as you wish.

Siren's Song

YOU WILL NEED TO GATHER:

*A medium length each of green,
mauve and blue wool
Floral perfume*

A perfect soul mate is possible for everyone, but for love magic to work effectively, you first need to love and believe completely in yourself. Reflect on that for a while, and then cast this spell at 7 o'clock on a Sunday evening. Gather together the three lengths of

wool and tie them end to end so they form one long strand. Spray a light mist of floral perfume around you and then loosely wrap the strand of wool around your waist. Look at your reflection in a mirror as you say:

> *'From the song of the sirens,*
> *With the call of the mermaid,*
> *I now open myself to receive true love*
> *And never will it fade.'*

Finish by rolling the strand of wool up in a ball and keeping it near your bed in a dresser drawer.

Goddess Deborah's

Favourite Potions and Enchanted Notions

One of my greatest joys is to rummage through
my precious collection of ancient recipes and
secret potions to find new and exciting ways of
weaving a little love magick.

On the following pages are some of my favourite
charms, potions and enchanted notions to help
you find romance, bring back a past love
or meet your perfect match.

Be My Valentine

YOU WILL NEED TO GATHER:

3 pieces of parchment or recycled paper
A green pencil
A small snip of your own hair

Whether searching for a soul mate, looking for a lost love, or happily married, we could all do with a bit of passion power. What better time to weave a little magic than Valentine's Day! In the days of ancient Rome, February 14th was celebrated as a holiday

festival for romance and engagement. The wife of Jupiter, the goddess Juno, would bestow her blessings on courting couples to bring good luck to any singles hunting for their ideal lovemate.

Ask Juno for some modern wizardry by casting this spell on the night before Valentine's Day. Write down the name of your intended lover on each of the three pieces of paper with a green pencil and sprinkle a little of your hair on top of each page. Roll the pieces up one by one and concentrate on attracting your lover toward you as you hold them near your chest and say these words:

> *'With goddess power so divine,*
> *I curl my locks as you do mine,*
> *One before and two behind,*
> *Be my only Valentine.'*

Forever After

YOU WILL NEED TO GATHER:

*A teaspoon each of cinnamon,
marjoram, ginseng, sage and basil
A wooden bowl
A sieve*

Every person you meet and every relationship you have is a lesson for your soul. Before you are ready to meet someone new, it is important to clear away any bitterness over a past relationship, especially if you have just been through a break-up or you have regrets. Throw your old worries to the wind with this great renewal ceremony.

At some time before the ceremony, mix and grind the herbs and spices together in a wooden bowl as you let go of negativity or any bitterness about the old relationship. Next, pour the mixture into a sieve so that only the finest powder is left. Discard the rest. Stand near an open window or go outside to a safe place and throw the magic mixture up in the air, while repeating this incantation:

> *'Here to the sacred wind*
> *Fly my worries and my past,*
> *Out with the old and in with the new,*
> *My true path is clear at last.'*

Please
Mr Postman

YOU WILL NEED TO GATHER:

A pink candle
A white candle
Light floral perfume
A medium-sized pink envelope

If your lover is out of town and you'd like to perk up his interest, cast this spell on the night of either a new or a full moon. Sit down at your writing table to write a letter and light one pink and one white

candle. Meditate for a few minutes while you think about the one you love. Imagine you are next to him, feeling very contented and happy. As you write your letter, open your mind and heart to let that happiness flow through you. Be spontaneous with what you say to him in the letter.

When you finish writing, spray the folded letter with a light floral perfume and put it into a medium-sized pink envelope. Hold it to your chest as you say:

> *'On this magic night*
> *Fly quickly my words and thoughts*
> *To reach the man I love.'*

Post the letter the next morning at 9 o'clock.

Baby Come Back

YOU WILL NEED TO GATHER:

A small taper candle
A pink or red rose thorn
Clove oil
A small red or purple silk drawstring bag

To help bring back an ex-lover, inscribe his initials with the thorn of a pink or red rose in the side of a small taper candle. (Use a candle that will burn down in fifteen or twenty minutes.) Then anoint the

candle with a drop or two of oil of clove. As you light the candle, visualise your ex-lover's face and repeat this incantation:

> *'This candle is my burning love for you*
> *As bright as the sacred sun.*
> *May this flame warm your spirit*
> *And let us soon be one.'*

Sit back in a comfortable position and gaze at the candle until it melts down into a puddle of wax. Allow the candle flame to go out naturally. When the wax has cooled right down and hardened, put it into the silk bag and tie up the drawstring. For extra attraction power, you can tie the bag to a pretty ribbon and wear it around your neck or place it near the phone for an hour or so each evening.

Perfect Reflection

If you are wondering what Mr or Ms Right will look like, cast a soul mate reflection spell by gathering a red candle in the evening on a Friday, the day of Venus. Go to a room in which you can see your reflection in a darkened window, light the candle and turn off all electric light.

Gaze at your own eyes and ask any question about your soul mate, such as, 'What will he look like?' Then close your eyes and turn away from the

window. After a few seconds, open your eyes and quickly look over your shoulder – you may see their reflection appearing in the window along with yours.

Food of Love
Edible Aphrodisiacs

LICORICE

This aromatic sweet is a very ancient aphrodisiac.

SAGE

This popular kitchen herb is often used in bath oils.

TRUFFLES

The best kind is from a wild mushroom-like fungus that grows in Europe. Expensive but very effective.

EGGS

Apparently many European gypsies feed their lovers a mixture of whipped raw eggs and sugar to keep up sexual stamina.

TIRAMISU

Not only does this famous Italian dessert taste divine, it is said to be a powerful aphrodisiac.

FO-TI-TIENG

An ancient Chinese herb that can be sipped in tea before lovemaking.

MUSHROOMS

Lightly cook mushrooms or serve them raw in a salad to arouse the passion within.

OYSTERS

Oysters are a sensuous and exotic addition to any romantic meal.

GINSENG

A well-known herb for stamina and sexuality. Can be taken as a tea or in a vitamin pill.

Tropical Delight

One of the most ancient and effective aphrodisiacs is the Polynesian kava root. Polynesian islanders use kava in important celebrations and love rituals; they either just nibble on the root or blend powdered kava with coconut milk.

The simplest way to make your own exotic love drink is to mix the following ingredients in a blender.

2 or 3 teaspoons powdered kava*
2 teaspoons olive oil
1 tablespoon soya lecithin or coconut granules
1 cup fresh water
½ cup soya milk

* If you can't find any kava root, you can use
sweetened cocoa powder as an excellent substitute.

Blend on high for one minute and you'll have
enough for 2–4 people.

French Kissing Wine

As we all know, the French are renowned for their prowess in both the kitchen and the bedroom. It is said that Josephine used this magic recipe to enchant her Emperor Napoleon. To make French Kissing Wine, mix together the following ingredients in a large bowl.

2 bottles Chablis
1 vanilla stick, chopped
a pinch ground cinnamon
1 rhubarb stick, chopped

Let the wine chill in the fridge for 2–3 hours and stir well as you say these words:

'Golden sun shine light divine,
Fill with love this wondrous wine.'

Strain the mixture through a clean cheesecloth and discard the solids. Pour the remaining liquid into a crystal or glass wine decanter to serve with lunch or dinner.

Quick-fix Love Charms

PUMPKIN PASSION

To make an ancient love charm, put seven pumpkin seeds into a small bag of yellow or white cotton. Tie the bag with a gold ribbon and carry it in your pocket or purse.

LEMON LOVE

Cut a heart-shaped piece of peel from a lemon. Place it on a windowsill and let it dry in the sun for seven days. Then wrap it up in a pink cloth and place it under your bed.

WISHBONE CHARM

To make a love wish come true, save the wishbone from a Christmas turkey and nail it onto your front door on New Year's Day.

TULIP TEASER

To help invite love into your house, keep tulip bulbs in a wooden box somewhere near your front door.

Aphrodisia Balm

YOU WILL NEED TO GATHER:

Rose essential oil
Neroli or orange essential oil
Ginger essential oil
One tablespoon of Vaseline (petroleum jelly)

Perfumes and scented body oils have been arousing lust and passion for centuries. This aphrodisia balm is a potent scent and quite expensive to make, but well worth it if you want to knock somebody's socks off.

On the night of a full or new moon, go to a private space in your home and put all your magic items on a flat surface. Undress and remain skyclad (witchs' term for naked) during the spell. Put six drops of rose oil, six drops of neroli (or orange) and one drop of ginger into a clean, small glass jar. Mix in a tablespoon of petroleum jelly while you visualise the person you want to attract. Repeat this incantation:

> *'Magic of the ancient gods,*
> *Serve me well this lunar night*
> *And send me love on every breath*
> *Of this enchanted scent.'*

Dab a little of the balm on your wrists and behind your ears. Store the remaining balm in the jar (with the lid twisted on tightly) in the fridge to keep it fresh.

Rose Power

Why wait for that special someone to send you flowers when you can weave your own spell with the Magic Rose of Love!

I have personally charged this red rose with a powerful enchantment. Touch the picture with your right hand, then visualise cuddling your loved one as you repeat these magic words:

> *'Roses are red,*
> *Violets are blue*
> *The touch of Venus*
> *Shall bring me to you.'*

For added power, place a photo of yourself or your loved one on top of the rose, close the book and leave it in your bedroom drawer for at least one night.

Colours
of Love

Every day of the week has its corresponding
magic colour. So, if you are meeting your lover,
or just want to exude a special attraction,
look up the day and wear something that
matches the corresponding shade.

MONDAY

Silver

TUESDAY

Red

WEDNESDAY

Green

THURSDAY

Purple

FRIDAY

Pink

SATURDAY

Dark Blue

SUNDAY

Gold

Crystal Magic

Some of my most powerful spells include the energy of crystals and gems. Not only are these stones bright and alluring, but each one contains special and magical attributes, helping you focus and strengthen enchantments for love and romance. Look up your star sign in the list opposite and find your matching love crystal.

Wash your crystal in spring water mixed with a pinch of salt. Dry it well with a clean white cloth and keep this magic crystal in your pocket or on your desk.

AQUARIUS aquamarine

ARIES garnet

CANCER moonstone

CAPRICORN malachite

GEMINI agate

LEO amber

LIBRA lapis lazuli

PISCES amethyst

SAGITTARIUS topaz

SCORPIO tourmaline

TAURUS turquoise

VIRGO carnelian

Moon Power

FULL MOON

For casting spells of love and high magic

NEW MOON

To begin a brand new relationship

WAXING OR GROWING MOON

To attract a soul mate or to strengthen a relationship

WANING OR DIMINISHING MOON

To end a relationship or to banish negative energy